Strong on the Outside, Dying on the Inside

*A Black Woman's Guide to
Finding Freedom from Depression*

by

Lisa M. Brown

Strong on the Outside, Dying on the Inside
A Black Woman's Guide to Finding Freedom from Depression
by Lisa M. Brown

Printed in the United States of America

ISBN 9781612155920

Unless otherwise indicated, Bible quotations are taken from the King James Version.

www.xulonpress.com

About the Author

Lisa M. Brown is a passionate and dynamic entrepreneur who, with the help of God, overcame depression to lead a thriving consulting business. As a business owner, daughter, sister, and mother of three, she brings her rich Christian heritage and experiences as a Black woman living in America to the very important issue of depression.

Lisa attained professional success early in her career and at the age of 35, became one of the youngest senior executives with the American Association of Homes and Services for the Aging, a Washington, D.C.-based trade association. She later went on to build Nonprofit HR Solutions, a fast-growing, trail-blazing consulting firm focused on meeting the human resources needs of nonprofit organizations.

More important than her professional success, Lisa is deeply committed to living out her faith in God in a meaningful way. She has been an active member of the music ministries of her churches in Toronto, Canada, where she grew up, as well as Washington, D.C. Not satisfied with just sitting in the pews, Lisa also served as business manager for the Howard Gospel Choir of Howard University, member of Greater Mount Calvary Holy Church under the leadership of Archbishop Alfred A. Owens, Jr., and as minister of music and praise team leader with the Bladensburg SDA Church. Lisa currently attends Bladensburg SDA Church where Noah L. Washington is the Pastor.

Lisa brings to this book her deeply personal and previously unspoken experience with depression. As a depression survivor, she now openly shares both the pains and triumphs associated with living with chronic sadness.

Strong on the Outside, Dying on the Inside is a very moving and beautifully written account of Lisa's anguish and strong determination to serve as a living testimony of God's amazing power to heal and restore. Her mission is help women – particularly those who consider themselves to be strong, Black women – get the freedom from depression that they desperately deserve.

For more information or to request Lisa as a speaker, visit *www.strongontheoutside.com.*

Acknowledgments

I wrote this book out of my own personal experience and by the inspiration of the Holy Spirit. I pray that it inspires you to break your silence and find the healing that God is ready and willing to give.

I want to especially acknowledge these very important people, without whom I would not be a living testimony today:

My mother, Norma Mattocks Brown, and my father,
Earle Brown, for your unwavering love, guidance
and support throughout my entire life.

My sons, Niles, Zachary and Marcus, for teaching me patience
and unselfishness. Without you I would have no earthly joy.

My immediate and extended family, especially my sisters,
Karen and Marcia, for being my first best friends.

My brother and friend, John Pearson, and my cousins, Errol Brown and Desmond Brown, for standing for me when I couldn't do it for myself.

Patty Hampton, for being my colleague, friend, and confidant. Without you, I would not be where I am professionally.

Kevin Alexander, for your support and encouragement throughout my never-ending writing journey.

Cheryl Ingraham, for inspiring me to transfer my pain to paper.

Henry Williams, for the powerful and prophetic words you've spoken over my life. You will never know what an impact you've had on me! (Thank you, Henry, for letting God use you to speak to me!)

Tony Mack, for being a wonderful listener and an even better friend.

Bobby Dunmore for helping me laugh so many times when I felt like crying. Your gift is not only as a wonderful hairstylist but also as an encourager and a preacher of the Word! Love ya, man!

Joan Steele, Avery Wilson Dixon, Sharon Vaz, Cheryl Ingraham and Nadine Cid, for being my "girls" and such wonderful listeners. (You talked me off the ledge so many times! Thank you! Love you always!)

My Bishop and Pastor for life, Bishop Alfred A. Owens, Jr. of Greater Mt. Calvary Holy Church. I can't thank you enough for taking the time to support my vision.

Pastor Noah Washington, Chaplain Robin Walker, Cheryl Drew and the Bladensburg SDA Church Music Ministry Team. Thank you for praying for me when I couldn't pray for myself.

Terrie Williams, for your amazing strength and the courage to tell your story. Thank you for inspiring me to tell mine.

Dr. Barbara Jones Warren, Dr. Freda Lewis-Hall, Sylvia Lackey Corcoran, LCSW, Dr. Lloyda Broomes Williamson, and Dr. Kumea Shorter-Gooden, for your willingness to share your expertise so freely. You will never know how much I have appreciated the privilege of learning from you.

My editor, Lee McAuliffe Rambo, for your wonderful editing skills.

Toni Riggs and the entire Xulon Press team,
for helping tell my story.

And most importantly, My Heavenly Father
for keeping for me a time such as this.

This book is dedicated to **every Black woman**
who, in her quest to be strong,
has found herself locked
in a prison of silence,
suffering from depression,
chronic sadness,
and
unspoken pain.

I pray that your walk
through the valley of despair
may soon be over
and that your return
to emotional,
mental
and
spiritual freedom
be ever near.

Contents

Introduction

Biblical/Contextual Reference

I Samuel 1: 5-10 (Recommended Reading, I Samuel 1:1-20)
(Today's New International Version)

Verse 5
But to Hannah, he [Elkanah] gave a double portion because he loved her, and the LORD had closed her womb.

Verse 6
Because the LORD had closed Hannah's womb, her rival kept provoking her in order to irritate her.

Verse 7
This went on year after year. Whenever Hannah went up to the house of the LORD, her rival provoked her till she wept and would not eat.

Verse 8
Her husband Elkanah would say to her, "Hannah, why are you weeping? Why don't you eat? Why are youdownhearted? Don't I mean more to you than 10 sons?"

B ut unto Hannah, he (Elkanah) gave a *worthy* portion – a double portion of the best of what he had. Hannah's husband provided her with everything she needed. She had a house, a chariot and a multitude of servants to do her every bidding. She didn't have to do her own laundry. She didn't have to worry about making healthy, balanced dinners after a long, hard day at work. She didn't even have to worry about paying bills or saving for retirement. Hannah was a kept woman! She wasn't broke. She wasn't struggling to make ends meet. She wasn't living paycheck to paycheck.

On the outside, Hannah was doing well and looking good. She had a husband who loved her and a close group of family and friends who supported her — well, all except for the "other wife," but we'll talk more about her later! She took annual pilgrimages to the house of the Lord at Shiloh, in keeping with her family's tradition. Hannah looked and played the part assigned to her, but she also carried a deep, unreachable pain that she couldn't talk about. As many of us do today, she learned to keep her game-face on and went about her business as though everything was okay.

Chances are, if you felt compelled enough to buy this book, you may have done or are doing the same thing. As strong, accomplished Black women, we have mastered the art of illusion. I say "illusion" because we've managed to con-vince everyone around us that we're God-fearing women who can handle any and everything you throw our way. We hold it down at work, sing in the choir and serve on the usher board at church, volunteer with the PTA, help the children with their homework, encourage our mates to pursue their dreams, and serve as a listening ear for our best girlfriends, sisters and mothers — sometimes all in the same day! But inside, we're broken and in pain – and will take our last breath before we let anyone know it. We're strong on the outside yet we're dying on the inside – mentally, emotionally, and spiritually – and no one seems to know.

Some of us are hurting from the time we wake up until the time we go to sleep. I'm not necessarily talking about physical pain here, although that's often the case when our mental and emotional health is not as it should be. I'm talking about being in pain because our minds, bodies and spirits are in desperate need of peace, healing and restoration.

In our desperation to hide our hurt and pain, some of us even feel as if we've lost our connection with God. We feel like He no longer hears us and so we stop praying, and then we feel guilty and ashamed for not talking to God and for not being able to get over our depression.

Hannah's story is as much about you and me as it is about her. Yes, you! You know, that got-it-all-together, rock-of-Gibraltar, never-let-'em-see-you- sweat you! As we journey through Hannah's story, and some of mine, I hope to empower you to let go of the pretenses and the burdens you've been carrying, to put your trust in God, and to actively seek an end to your days of perpetual darkness and despair.

Webster's dictionary defines depression as "sad feelings of gloom and inadequacy." Well, it's time to lay down that sadness, gloom and inadequacy. It's time to lay down that gameface, girl. It's time to surrender your pain, sadness and feelings of hopelessness, and trade them in for that joy and peace that *only* God can give. It's time for you to get your life back!

Through this book, I hope to help you break free from the weeks, months and, in some cases, years of pain that you've experienced but nobody knows about. I hope you will allow yourself to cry, pray, and talk your way into a new place in life, one that will allow you to release all that has been burdening you and preventing you from living your life to the fullest.

If you're tired of the perpetual sadness and darkness that seems to have overtaken your life, tired of living in a spirit of depression, repression and oppression, and are ready to live again – I mean really live again — then keep reading! Find a quiet space, grab yourself a box of tissues, have your Bible close by and get ready to purge the spirit of depression from your life once and for all! I got your back. More importantly, God has your heart and mind, and He's ready and waiting for you to get back to a life of purpose and joy. Come on, let's get started!

Chapter 1

Hannah's Story

> *In her deep anguish*
> *Hannah prayed to the LORD,*
> *weeping bitterly.*

> *1 Samuel 1:10*
> *Today's New International Version*

Have you ever experienced pain so profound that you felt you weren't going to make it? Not physical pain, but emotional pain. Heartbreak. Sadness. Chronic despair. Have you lost your appetite for the simple pleasures of life, like going for a walk, or watching the sun set, or listening to the laughter of a small child? Are you so burdened in your spirit that you can't sleep or eat? Are you living with an emptiness that money, clothes and even loved ones can't seem to fill? Well, that was Hannah's story.

In the Bible, I Samuel 1: 1-20 tells the short but poignant story of Hannah. She was one of two wives of Elkanah the Ephraimite. Elkanah's *other* wife was Penninah. Hannah was barren and unable to bear children for her husband. Penninah had many sons and daughters with Elkanah. What made it worse, Penninah never missed an opportunity to remind Hannah of her condition. In Hannah's time, a woman's worth was measured by how many children she could bear. Hannah had neither children nor self-worth. Yet despite her infertility, Hannah's husband gave her a double portion of what he gave to Penninah simply because he loved her.

Hannah had all the comforts of life, but she was miserable because she was childless. Penninah provoked Hannah repeatedly about her condition and eventually drove her to despair. Hannah became depressed. She couldn't talk about her feelings with her husband, despite his many efforts to console her and assure her of his love for her. She couldn't talk about it with her mother or best friends. She probably couldn't even talk about it with her spiritual leader. Instead, *without saying a word*, Hannah removed herself from Penninah's constant ridicule and what was an unbearable situation. In total desperation, she pleaded with God for guidance and relief from her barrenness. She eventually found herself at the temple in the company of Eli, the priest. Eli counseled her – although he really thought she was drunk. He didn't fully understand her situation. There, at the temple, after agonizing before the Lord, Hannah found release from the debilitating spirit of sadness that had been ruling her life. And, hearing her prayers, God blessed her with the gift of a son, Samuel.

There's so much of you and me in Hannah's story — so many lessons about pain and pretense, hopelessness and hope, faith and deliverance. I want so much for you to know that, just like Hannah, you can experience radical, life-altering change! You don't have to accept depression as your destiny! What you are experiencing now is not what or how your life must always be. I know. I've been where you are. And, by God's grace and with professional help, I found freedom from the shackles of darkness and despondency that had me bound. And so can you!

Let's look at Hannah's story a little more closely and the process she went through to receive deliverance from depression. We know that in the culture of Hannah's day not having a child – especially a male child – meant having no security in one's old age. Both in the community and within her family, a woman without a child had to live with the stigma of being cursed by God. Hannah's barrenness represented emptiness, physical and emotional. And with that emptiness, came a lack of self-worth that all the gifts in the world couldn't fill. Hannah was hurting.

You may share Hannah's plight. As a young woman, you may have dreamed of becoming a mother and having a family of your own. You may have taken for granted that motherhood would come to you as naturally as womanhood or being Black. I can only imagine the pain of wanting children but being unable to give birth to your own.

According to the 2002 National Survey of Family Growth by the Department of Health and Human Services, roughly 10.5 percent of Black women ages 15 to 44 are affected by infertility.[1] That means roughly one in 10 Black women in this country is unable to conceive naturally. That's a lot of women in your church, in your community and in your workplace who may be affected by this condition.

Being a mother of three sons myself, I can't begin to fully understand the agony you may feel. Truthfully, I can only listen, offer support and pray that God grants you peace with your present situation and that, if it's His will, He will give you the desires of your heart. Or maybe you're already a mother, having given birth to as many children as you chose to bear without ever encountering the challenges and stresses that infertility can bring. If that's your situation, not being able to conceive a child simply isn't your testimony.

But, as compelling as that portion of Hannah's story is, this book isn't about motherhood or infertility. It's not about being a kept woman or having to share your man, although I could write volumes on that topic! It's not even about jealousy (Penninah's), envy (Hannah's) or favoritism (Elkanah's).

Hannah's story is about being in pain and what we as women — famously strong Black women, mothers and non-mothers, young and old, financially stable and unstable, formally educated and educated by the lessons of life — often go through in dealing and not dealing with our depression.

Let's break this down some more. Look at I Samuel 1:6 again. Penninah, Elkanah's other wife, knew about Hannah's infertility. The Word of God tells us that Penninah had many children by her husband. Knowing what Hannah was going through because she could not conceive, Penninah, her rival, provoked her. Simply put, Penninah got on Hannah's last nerve! She tried to break Hannah's spirit. And, quite honestly, she almost did. Penninah knew that Hannah was in pain emotionally and possibly physically because of her barren state, and yet she kept on provoking her. Year after year after year, Penninah did all that she could to remind Hannah of what she didn't have: children for her husband.

Now as disturbing as it may be to us today that Hannah and Penninah were sharing a husband, that's not what this book is about either. I thank God that we live in a different time when we're no longer expected to be one of many wives to one husband, like the women of Hannah and Penninah's day. And while some of us may be involuntarily sharing our men with women we know nothing about, this story isn't about that either! If you are married to a man who is involved with another woman (or women) and you *know* about it, I pray that you find the inner strength to acknowledge what's happening and take care of yourself both physically and emotionally. If you have children, it is even more important that you do what you have to do to ensure your health and theirs. I know that it's easy for people to say "Girl, you need to get up outta there!" but only you and God know your situation. That said, you need to get up outta there! Seriously.

I'm going to say this and then I'm going to move on: sharing your husband with another woman is *not* what God has ordained for you. Ever! I don't care if you think you're doing it for the children, or to maintain your current lifestyle, or because you're worried about what folks will say about you, or because you think you have the upper hand because at least he comes home to you at night! Trust and believe, girl-friend, you can and must know that you can do better! 'Nuf said!

So here's the *real* issue. As many of us strong Black women do when we're in pain, Hannah said nothing about what she was going through — absolutely nothing! Look at your Bible. Review the text. There is absolutely no evidence that Hannah spoke to anyone. There's no evidence that Hannah got in Penninah's face, cursed her out or told her about herself, as much as she may have wanted to. Come on. Let's be real here. If you or I were in that situation, we probably would! Some of us, because of our anger and confusion about our depression, have cursed people out for far less. Many of us have pretty short fuses, and we can sometimes be too quick to give folks a piece of our minds. We get that oh-no-she-didn't! attitude in a New- York minute, and but for our good, Christian upbringing, we'd probably take some folks out! Sadly, we're hurting and sometimes hurt others with what we say and how we act. I'm not making any excuses. I'm just saying.

Hannah took a different approach. She didn't respond to Penninah with anger. She wasn't confrontational. She didn't even complain to her husband, although she would have been well within her rights to do so. Instead, Hannah internalized her pain, wept and stopped eating.

Let's stay right here for a moment. Right here at the internalizing and the crying, and the loss of interest in things that used to bring us joy. Don't miss this! This is the part of Hannah's story that you have to get. I truly believe that by understanding Hannah's response to her pain and sadness, you can — with the help of God, a good therapist and a loving circle of family and friends — unlock the door to your depression. I believe that taking the time to study Hannah's life and her subsequent deliverance will set you on a journey to understanding and finding freedom from the spirit of depression that has consumed your life.

Before we go any further, let's pray:

Dear Lord, I thank you for my sistah whose hands are holding this book. I thank you for her willingness to embark on the process of breaking free from the spirit of depression that has become all too familiar to her. I pray even now that she will begin to imagine what her life will look like once You deliver her, and that something within her, something she thought was dead, comes back alive. I pray against any spirit of doubt that may cause her to become discouraged. I pray against any person that may try to provoke her or keep her bound. We know your Word is true and with You all things are possible. We believe You for healing, right now Lord, in the name of Jesus, we pray. Amen.

Chapter 2
Hannah Was Depressed. Are You?

"I almost let go...
I felt like I just couldn't take life anymore
My problems had me bound
Depression weighed me down..."

Kurt Carr,
Gospel Recording Artist

B efore we move forward, let's re-focus. Remember, our goal is to help you get free from the spirit of depression that has taken over your life. Don't get distracted. Stay with me!

I don't want you to focus on motherhood or even man-sharing! As important as these issues are, they are subjects for another day and time. And, for the moment, I don't even want you to focus on what led you to feeling depressed in the first place. I want you to focus on you and getting back your mental, emotional and spiritual freedom! I want you to focus on what it's going to feel like to not be in pain anymore; to not feel sad and despondent day in and day out. Once you get back to where you should be — and you will — you will find the strength and courage to deal with the other circumstances in your life. But first we need to deal with your depression.

What is depression anyway? According to the National Alliance on Mental Illness (NAMI), "depression is a common and highly treatable disorder affecting some 17 to 20 million Americans annually."[2] Clinical depression, the medical term for depression, generally lasts for two or more weeks and involves disturbances in mood, concentration, sleep, activity level, interests, appetite and behavior.

Some common symptoms of depression include: persistent sadness, emptiness or irritability; major changes (mainly losses) in sleep, appetite or energy; difficulty thinking, concentrating or remembering; lack of interest in or pleasure from activities that you once enjoyed; persistent physical symptoms such as headaches, digestive disorders and chronic pain that don't respond to treatment; and suicidal thoughts. Does any of this sound familiar?

If you have experienced any of these symptoms for more than a few weeks, you very likely are suffering from depression. And, if you are, you're not alone. It is believed that thousands of Black women suffering from depression go undiagnosed or under-diagnosed every year.

Multiple factors contribute to inadequate treatment of depression in the Black community, and numerous myths and stigmas surround depression. Many African Americans fear meeting with a mental health professional for a variety of reasons — including fear that others will find out that they are receiving mental health treatment and will put them down, fear that they will be experimented on and fear that they will be labeled "crazy." Some mental health professionals are not culturally competent and are not aware of how depression may show itself in Black women and therefore miss making an accurate diagnosis. These are just a few reasons that so many Black women receive no treatment for depression.

Depression can affect anyone, regardless of age, gender, race, socioeconomic status or religion. Depression affects Black women and White women, men and children, rich and poor, Baptists and Methodists, Pentecostals and non-denominationals, atheists and agnostics. It is an equal opportunity condition!

There are several types of depression that are distinguished by their key features, duration and severity of symptoms. Most forms are defined by the Diagnostic and Statistical Manual of Mental Disorders (DSM), a reference publication produced by the American Psychiatric Association and used by mental health professionals.

Major depressive disorder, also known as major depression or clinical depression, is usually reflected in depressed mood or a noticeable decrease in interest or pleasure in all or most activities for at two weeks and is accompanied by at least five (or more) of the following that occur nearly every day: significant weight loss when not dieting or weight gain or decrease or increase in eating; difficulty sleeping or increase in sleeping; psychomotor agitation (unintended and purposeless movements that are created by worry) and psychomotor retardation (decreased thoughts and movements caused by mental tension); loss of energy; feelings of worthlessness or inappropriate guilt; decreased ability to think or concentrate; repeated thoughts of death or thoughts of suicide or a specific plan for suicide.

Dysthymic disorder, also called dysthymia, is manifested by a depressed mood lasting at least two years and is accompanied by at least two of the following: decrease or increase in eating; difficulty sleeping or increase in sleeping; low energy or fatigue; low self-esteem; difficulty concentrating or making decisions; and feeling hopeless Generally, this type of depression is characterized by persistent but less severe depressive symptoms than major depression.

Mania or manic depression, also known as bipolar disorder, includes periods of mania and depression. A manic episode consists of a persistent elevated or irritable mood that is extreme and typically lasts for at least one week. At least three other features also are present. These include inflated self-esteem or self-importance; decreased need for sleep; being more talkative than usual or feeling compelled to keep talking; experiencing racing thoughts or ideas; being easily distracted; experiencing an increase in goal-oriented activity (social, work, school, sexual); excessive movement; or excessive involvement in potentially risky pleasurable behavior (overspending, careless sexual activity, unwise business investments, etc.).

Symptoms of most of these types of depression can be severe enough to require hospitalization to prevent harm to oneself or others. Depression may include psychotic features such as hallucinations and delusions.[3] Undoubtedly, depression is a serious, authentic illness.

The good news is that 80 to 90 percent of individuals diagnosed with depression can be effectively treated and returned to their normal daily activities and feelings. So then why do so many of us fail to get the help that we need? According to NAMI, only 12 percent of affected African American women seek help or treatment for depression.[4]

According to BlackWomensHealth.com, "many African-American women do not get treatment because of a widespread belief that depression is evidence of personal weakness and is not a legitimate health problem." Depression has nothing to do with weakness! It's not a "mood" or a "phase" that someone can just snap out of. It is a major health concern that can affect anyone at any point in life. And, like any other major health condition, it should be addressed head on with the guidance of qualified professionals, compassionate spiritual guides, and a circle of supportive family and friends.

Lloyda Broomes Williamson, M.D., a psychiatrist at the University of Alabama, often educates individuals in her practice and in her seminars by telling them this: "Seeking professional help for depression is a strength. Often a problem will improve if you have it checked out and treated sooner instead of later. Depression is like that. If it is untreated, it can become a worse depressive episode."

I don't know if Hannah was a Black woman; some might argue that she was. That's not the point. What is important is that Hannah was depressed. And like many of us today, she learned to bury her sadness deep within her and suffer in silence. Hannah was in pain and wouldn't talk about it. I did the same thing. Chances are you have too.

Not only was Hannah chronically sad and despondent but she also wouldn't eat. Eating represents one of those things that normally bring us pleasure. It is often the center of our most meaningful family gatherings and connects us to our past and present. We gather over meals to celebrate, to conduct business, to socialize and even when someone dies! Eating is what many of us do not only to sustain ourselves but also to connect with others.

Often when we stop eating, we stop doing other things too. We stop reaching out. We stop sharing what's happening within us and, instead, in an effort to protect ourselves and sometimes others, close ourselves off from those who care about us the most.

When was the last time you went out for a relaxing meal with a friend or family member? When was the last time you took a moment to savor the food you were eating or enjoy the sweet or spicy smells coming from the kitchen? Maybe you're gifted with fabulous culinary skills and used to be known for whipping up a four-course meal that no one could refuse. When was the last time you did that? Can't remember? Been that long, huh? Not good. What else have you stopped doing? I'll let you answer that for yourself.

Now if you're anything like me, you probably can afford to miss a few meals! I've never been blessed to hear anyone say, "Girl, you're getting so skinny! You need to eat!" But I'm not talking about cutting back on a couple of meals so you can shed a few pounds to fit into that cute little black dress in your closet.

I'm talking about living with the kind of perpetual sadness and despair that cause you to stop doing things that once brought you joy and pleasure. I'm talking about being in a place where your mental, physical, emotional and spiritual health gets so off-balance that you experience long periods of emptiness and sorrow that take hold in your life and won't let go.

While we're on the subject of food, it is important to note that eating disorders are one of the most common manifestations of depression. When we are depressed, we often either deprive ourselves of the sustenance and nutrition needed to be physically and emotionally healthy, or we overeat as a way of comforting ourselves or numbing our pain. Either scenario is not good or healthy. If you find yourself under- or overeating, pretending to eat or lying about eating, eating very little or eating excessively large portions of food, or realizing extreme weight gain or losses, I strongly encourage you to seek professional help. There are counselors, therapists and online resources available to help you deal with any eating disorders you may be experiencing.

Although the Bible doesn't speak to this specifically, I'm guessing that Hannah probably couldn't sleep much either. Have you stopped sleeping through the night? Do you find yourself going to bed early, waking up late and still feeling tired? Do you find yourself tossing and turning at night, unable to rest because your mind and spirit are weighed down by your unspoken pain? Do you feel overwhelmed at the thought of getting out of bed every morning and facing the challenges of life?

Sleep disorders or disturbances often are at their worst during periods of depression. Both insomnia and over-sleeping are common symptoms of depression. According to WebMD.com, "Insomnia and depression often go hand in hand. Although just 15 percent of people with depression sleep too much, as many as 80 percent of people have trouble falling asleep or staying asleep when they are depressed." According to Stanford University research psychologist Tracy Kuo, Ph.D., "Chronic sleep loss can lead to a loss of pleasure in life, and is one of the hallmarks of depression. When people can't sleep, they often become anxious about not sleeping. Anxiety increases the potential for becoming depressed."

I remember often being anxious when I was suffering from depression. I would anticipate the very worst about a given situation and begin to believe that it had actually hap-pened. I would become highly stressed at the possibility and that anxiety would turn into more feelings of sadness, despondency and hopelessness. I would break out in hives, feel my chest tightening, and have headaches and stomach aches. I later learned that there is a medical term for what I was experiencing: somatization. Somatization "is the process by which psychologic distress is expressed as physical symptoms. Somatization is an unconscious process."[5] It is a process by which mental and emotional stresses become physical. The notable changes that you may be experiencing in your body are not a figment of your imagination. They are real. Our mind and body share a very close, intertwined relationship. For me, the cycle of physical symptoms and mental and emotional stress repeated over and over and became almost torturous. It was like a bad movie playing in slow motion, one I could never seem to stop.

During my worst bouts of depression, I was often also completely unable to sleep at night. I would lie awake, staring at the ceiling, listening to myself rehearse all of the negative aspects of my life that I believed would never get better. In the silence of the night, my thoughts seemed louder, darker, more depressing. I began to internalize those negative feelings, driving myself even further into depression. It became a vicious, unending cycle, day and night, night and day.

I truly believe that Hannah was depressed. Go back and read the story. She was devastated by her inability to have a child, and her world grew dark around her because of it. Life around her seemed to go on as usual. Her family planned their annual trips to the countryside. Penninah kept having baby after baby. And even though Elkanah continued to shower Hannah with gifts and attention, Hannah's heart, mind and spirit were broken. She was sad and depressed and yet spoke to no one about it. No one. Not her mama, not her best girl-friend, not her pastor – not even her husband. Instead, she suffered silently.

If I do nothing else for you, I want to encourage you to break your silence. No, don't break it! Smash it into pieces! Tell yourself, despite what you may have heard growing up or told yourself as an adult, that silence isn't always golden. *There is absolutely no honor in silence when you are depressed.* None. There's no honor in holding on to your pain. You may have come to believe the myth that we Black women can handle just about anything you throw our way. But, believe me, depression is not one of those things!

There's no grand prize for not taking care of yourself, suffering sleepless nights, losing your passion for life or being emotionally and mentally absent from those you love and who love you. That's what depression does to you. It robs you of life, joy and peace. And the worst thing: It does it slowly and often painfully.

Suffering in silence doesn't make you a stronger, more authentic Black woman. Quite honestly, the only thing you may have earned is more pain and more sadness. It's time to let that go, girlfriend. Now, today, it's time.

I *so* want you to release the pain and sadness that have been plaguing you. I want you to start right here and now. No more living with how badly you've been feeling. This is not the life God has intended for you! It's simply not. The Word of God says very clearly that the Lord wants us to "prosper and be in good health." (*3 John 1:2, KJV*). Living a depressed life is neither prospering nor being in good health. I'm no pastor, but I believe that prosperity in this context has less to do with money and more to do with disposition – spiritual, emotional, mental and physical, rather than material possessions. You can have all the money and stuff in the world, but if you don't have good health – especially mental health — you have nothing. Your mind is your body's control center and, if you are not able to achieve a place of mental balance and prosperity, it becomes very, very difficult to achieve and sustain good physical, emotional and even spiritual prosperity.

Am I striking a nerve? Hitting a little too close to home? Am I all up in your business? I hope so! And even though you may have been depressed for so long that you don't even remember what life looked and felt like B.D. (before depression), I declare to you today that you *will* find restoration for your mind, soul, and spirit! Not because I said so, but because you're sick and tired of being sick and tired. I know you are. More importantly, because God is able to heal your mind and spirit! He is able not only to heal and restore you but also to give you a life filled with joy and peace. He is! He really is!

My sole purpose for writing this book and sharing my own pain with you is to help you get your life back! You can do it! But before you do, let's pray:

Dear God: You say in Your Word that You have not given us a spirit of fear but of love, power and a sound mind! I'm standing on Your Word today, on behalf of my sistah who has found herself worn down from indescribable sadness. I need You right now God, to give her sound mind and a peace that will pass all of her understanding. Break the spirit of depression that has taken hold of her and won't let her go! Even now, dear God, she is weary and needs your strength. Help me to stand in the gap for her until she gets her breakthrough. Assure her of the joy that you have waiting for her. Keep her together, oh God, until she can get it together! I'm believing in You for her victory even now! In Jesus' name I pray. Amen.

Chapter 3
I'm a Strong Black Woman! I Got This.

꙳꙳꙳

"I don't want to walk on water anymore.
But if I don't, who will do it for me?"

— *Unknown African American Woman*

O kay, so let's deal with this strong Black woman thing. As Black women, we take great pride in our ability to bear the burdens of our children, families, communities and sometimes our entire race without stumbling or falling, no matter the weight that is pressed on us. After all, we endured the vicious passage from our ancestral homeland of Africa to the shores of America, the Caribbean and Europe; survived the horrors and brutality of slavery; persevered through seg- regation and discrimination; and achieved unprecedented economic, political and educational heights against all odds.

As Black *Christian* women, we have the added blessing of an unwavering belief that God will hold us up on every leaning side regardless of the valleys and circumstances that we find ourselves in. As part of our Christian ethos, we're taught from an early age that God will not give us more than we can bear. We're taught to count it all joy when we encounter various trials, knowing that the testing of our faith produces endurance. *(James 1:2)* I believe that. I really do. But that same belief can sometimes lead us to believe that depression and long periods of emptiness and sadness are necessary conditions of life to be endured and not overcome. "What doesn't kill you makes you stronger," right? After all, if Jesus endured all that He did for us, how dare we complain about the hardships we face in our individual lives? And so, in an effort to show our commitment to being good Christians, we tell ourselves that depression, among other things, is our cross to bear. Rather than feel guilty for complaining, like a woman giving birth to a child in days of old, we bear down and endure our pain as a demonstration of our faith, strength and internal fortitude.

Part of the problem is that ironically, as strong Black women, many of us are not really in touch with what's going on inside of us. We're not in touch with our inner selves or our emotions despite being full of emotion! And full of emotion, we are! Don't get me wrong. I think that's one of the most beautiful things about being a Black woman. We can be emotional without apology. We laugh hard, we love hard, we cry hard — and many times we also hurt hard. We often look at women of other races with curiosity because they appear too controlled, tight and restrained. Yet, ironically, in our attempts to be strong, we routinely suppress our need to show fear when we are afraid, to show pain when we are hurting, to cry when we are sad and to seek help when we are in need. And by not dealing with our hurt, pain and fear we find ourselves in conflict with ourselves and, many times, solidly on the path to depression.

Charisse Jones and Kumea Shorter-Gooden, PhD, who wrote the award-winning *Shifting: The Double Lives of Black Women in America* aptly refer to this crisis as the Sisterella Complex: "a manifestation of depression that is all too common in Black American women today." They describe Sisterella as "the Black woman who honors others but denies herself." She's a high achiever who works unceasingly "to promote, protect, and appease others." And because "her identity is confused, her personal goals are deeply buried, and she shrinks inwardly, she becomes depressed, sometimes severely so."[6] Jones and Shorter-Gooden go on to describe Sisterella as a silent sufferer who turns inward rather than act out. "She may feel angry but she beats up on herself rather than the world. She experiences excessive guilt; she feels worthless and unworthy; she puts herself down. She takes on the expectations and demands of her family, her job and the larger society, but doesn't push in turn for the support, nurturance, and caring that she needs."[7] Sound at all familiar?

Why do we take on everyone else's issues but never deal with our own? Because we're strong Black women, right? That's what we do. And despite our Sisterella complexes, we're often the backbones of our communities, churches and families. We come from generations of women who've had to hold it all together even when everything was falling apart! We come from a long history of overcoming every obstacle in our way. And so, despite the setbacks and struggles that we've encountered generation after generation, we've managed to raise our children, keep our communities together, serve in our churches, achieve success in our careers, build businesses, and graduate with bachelor's and advanced degrees at unprecedented rates. We're holding more political positions of power than ever before, and we're taking even more prominent roles in the pulpits of many of our churches. By all accounts, we're doing it!

But in fact, according to Kumea Shorter-Gooden, "our external success belies our internal struggles." And being strong Black women often comes with a heavy price. We carry what Barbara Jones Warren, PhD, a professor and clinical nursing specialty director at Ohio State University, calls "triple jeopardy." "We, despite our strides in business, education, politics, and religion, live in a majority-, male-dominated society that often does not fully value our ethnicity, culture and gender. We also carry the burden of not showing our pain because we have been conditioned to think that pain and suffering are things to be endured." How many times have you heard, "Girl, just suck it up. You'll be okay."

Being strong Black women also makes it hard to acknowledge that we have a problem with depression. How can we be strong, running stuff *and* depressed? How can we be strong and admit to suffering from what we understand as weakness? How can we not feel ashamed about our feelings of perpetual pain and sadness when everyone around us – including our families, churches and colleagues – believe and expect that we can handle everything?

To complicate things further, Dr. Shorter-Gooden says that being women of faith also can significantly impact our willingness to face and seek treatment for our depression. "We pray about our depression but then feel guilty when prayer doesn't feel like enough. We internalize the messages that we hear from the pulpit, our families and society that say if you are a 'good Christian,' you don't need treatment for depression — just prayer and 'true commitment' to God." We receive the message that if we are suffering from depression, it's because we are not strong enough in our faith and our belief in God's healing power is called into question. At the risk of getting on the bad side of a whole lot of good church folk, I say not so!

We need to stop drinking our own Kool-Aid and feeding ourselves lies about what it means to be strong, Black, female and Christian! We've somehow bought into the myth that as Black women we're not supposed to break down and fall apart or show that we are in pain and full of despair. We've bought into the myth that we need to be nurturing more than we need to be nurtured. We've fooled ourselves into believing that as long as we take care of our families and our careers, are active in our churches, and give back to our communities, we've arrived and we're okay even when we know that we're not. In reality, many of us find ourselves having lost our sense of self — for weeks, months and sometimes years — while caring for everything and everyone but ourselves.

Being a depression survivor, I wholly endorse the counsel that Charisse Jones and Kumea Shorter-Gooden give in *Shifting*. They encourage us to tell our friends, family, colleagues and loved ones that we need their love, support, and affirmation as much as they need the same thing from us. We need to feel comfortable with the idea and with telling those closest to us that our lives are valuable and that we need and deserve to be happy, healthy and fulfilled. That said, we first have to believe it ourselves. That's very difficult to do when we're depressed.

Let me keep it real! I did what thousands of Black women do every day. I took my job as a strong Black woman very seriously. I made sure that I was smarter, better and more prepared than my colleagues. I made sure to dress well and speak well in public settings. I didn't take any stuff from folks who thought they could dismiss me because of my race or gender. And I always took great pride in shocking folks with the notion that my race and gender had very little to do with what I could do! You know that thing that happens when folks say, "Oh wow! You're so smart and articulate too!" Why is that always such a surprise? Why? I tried to do everything with excellence because I was a Black woman and I always wanted to represent well. But those high expectations created a tremendous amount of pressure for me, especially when my depression was at its worst. How could I be that got-it-all-together sistah when I was feeling a mess inside? It felt nearly impossible.

That same pressure to be strong also drove me to remain silent about my depression. I couldn't be a strong Black woman *and* be depressed. That was an oxymoron! My career was soaring. I was living the big corporate success story, jet-setting back and forth on business every week between New York and Washington, D.C., trying to be all things to all people but myself. I had just had my second child, and I thought I had it all together because I could afford a live-in nanny, an apartment on the upper east side of Manhattan *and* a house in the suburbs of D.C. By everyone's standards – even my own – I was fairly successful in my little world; making an impressive salary, building my little family, traveling around the country. The truth is: I was livin' large and in pain. I mean, in pain. And I was afraid to let anyone see that I really didn't have it all together. And, like Hannah and probably like you, I told no one.

Every once in a while, my husband, like Elkanah, would say: "What's wrong, Lisa? Why are you crying? Everything alright? And, because I was afraid to show my hurt and pain, I would just say, "Yeah, everything is okay." I would bite back my tears, put a smile on my face and just keep on going. But when I was alone at home or in my car, I was a mess! I think I probably cried every day for five years straight. And, despite my professional success, I had no sense of self-worth. I felt unworthy of my professional achievements. I felt alone and afraid.

Because of my depression, there were times I wasn't the best wife, mother, sister or friend. My depression affected my relationships with husband and children, my family and my closest friends. I wasn't there for them like I should have been. I was physically present, but often emotionally absent. It's very hard to be your best when you are empty emotionally! But I didn't have the time to fall apart. How could I? I was vice president of my growing department at work. I was trying to build a consulting business. I was raising a family and serving in the music ministry at my church. If that wasn't enough, I came from a long line of proud, strong Jamaican women who had endured all sorts of adversity and had overcome. How could I dare complain about my plight? Doing so would be an insult to all the women in my family who had endured far more with far less.

Yet, the person who couldn't hold it together in private wasn't the person whom everyone knew me to be in public. Everyone knew and depended on me to be strong, outspoken, got-it-all-together Lisa — my family, friends, employer and even my church. And so, I did what hundreds of thousands of other strong, Black women do. I played the part assigned to me.

That's what Hannah did too. If Hannah were alive today, she probably would have played the role of wife, church member, sorority sister, homeowners' association president, community activist, member of this, member of that. Every year she would have gone to the family reunion, on the yearly vacation to Martha's Vineyard, or on the trip to the country to visit Big Ma. She probably would have attended her church's annual convocation and served on a committee or two. Sound familiar? But when everyone went their way and the activities of the day died down, Hannah would have taken off her mask, laid her game- face down and, according to I Samuel 1:10, she would be "in bitterness of soul."

Are you smiling in public but falling apart in private? Not able to hold it all together, yet not able to tell a soul? For years, I tried to hold it all together, striving harder and harder to numb my pain rather than face it. I was never a drinker, a smoker or a gambler, and I didn't really party that much. But, give me a few hours, and I could do some serious damage in a mall! I called it therapy shopping! Yeah, right. Actually, my real vice was work. It became my drug of choice, my tranquilizer. It got me through the day — until the next day when I needed another fix.

Don't get me wrong. I was grateful for the success I had experienced in my career. By the time I was 35, I was a vice president with a major, national trade association in Washington, D.C. I had my corner office, my rubber tree plant and the respect of my colleagues and staff, but I was dying inside, absolutely dying.

It never dawned on me to get off the fast track and take care of myself. I never gave myself permission not to have it all together. I also never gave myself permission to face my depression. I didn't name it or claim it! Instead, like so many other Black women do, I just kept on going. It was crazy. Absolutely ridiculous that, despite my success at work, my position of leadership at church, and my loving circle of family and friends, I never sought help.

It was a few years before I was able to face my depression and finally get the help that I needed. I finally got tired of wearing my strong Black woman mask. I found a wonderful, compassionate African American therapist in Washington, D.C. who, with her soothing voice and her amazing capacity to listen and hear, guided me back to a place of healing. Every week for an hour, I was able to find that safe place where I could empty myself of my pain, hurt and sadness. After the first few sessions, I started to count down the days and hours when I would be back in my therapist's office again. With all the skill and experience of a psychologist and the comforting touch of an aunt, she was able to help me draw out and face my pain. It was a hard road to travel. I had to face some stuff from my past that I didn't realize was affecting my present. I had to deal with my insecurities and my fears and my pain. And you do, too. Getting therapy is a key part of your healing.

I have to admit: I was anxious about going to therapy at first. Did it mean I was crazy? Was something wrong with me? How could I go to therapy without anyone knowing? I worried about someone finding out and concluding that I couldn't hold it all together. Ironically, I couldn't! That's exactly why I needed to get help. What was worse, though, was that my depression had me feeling so badly about myself that I didn't really believe therapy would help; my depression felt like a forgone conclusion. I was sad and in despair and that's just the way it was going to be…

I share this with you because you may be feeling the same way. Like your sadness is so far gone and your life so empty and without joy, that no one or no thing can fix it. That is so not true. Your walk may be through the valley of depression but that's not where you are going to stay. The Holy Spirit is here to comfort you. The Holy Spirit can and will restore your soul. But you have to trust that He will. You also have to believe that your present life is not all there is to living. We are not put on this earth to be sad, despondent and empty. We're not here to merely exist and survive through one depressed day after another. God does not intend for your life to be this way. We're here to live life and live it abundantly! Abundantly well. Being depressed and living abundantly well do not jibe. You've got to know that.

So, strong Black woman, with all of your fortitude and determination, set it in your mind to deal with your depression. You've dealt with some major stuff in your life. Somehow, you've been able to dig deep and find the strength to deal with life's challenges. Now, I want you to go back within yourself and find whatever strength you have to do just one thing: Tell God that you want to get better. That you need to get better, first for you and then for those you love!

Come on, sis. God is able and so are you! Let's pray:

Dear God: Thank you for making me a Black woman. Thank you for giving me the fortitude to endure the many trials and tribulations that have come my way. Right now, Lord, I need that same determination and strength to face my depression. I'm tired of the sadness and the pain. I'm tired of looking strong but feeling weak. I need Your power. Mine has run out. Help me God, as only you can, in Jesus' name. Amen.

Chapter 4

Letting Go and Letting God

⮑:❀:⮐

"Save me, O God, for the waters have threatened my life.
I have sunk in deep mire, and there is no foothold;
I have come into deep waters, and a flood overflows me.
I am weary with my crying; my throat is parched;
My eyes fail while I wait for my God."

Psalms 69:1-3, KJV

I applaud you for not putting this book down and giving into the fear and anxiety you may experience as you face your depression. The anxiety that you may be feeling is normal. You've taken an important yet difficult step by acknowledging your pain and getting yourself in a position to do something about it. Now you need to begin to identify and let go of that thing or series of things that took you down this long, winding road to the valley of sadness and despair.

51

Let me be really clear here. I'm not a psychologist, a psychiatrist or a therapist and I don't play one on TV! What I am is a living testimony to the value of good therapy and God's ability to heal depression. In my quest for healing, I tried a number of things, from prayer to positive self-talk to massage and gospel-music therapy (not at all a science but it worked for me!), to regular visits to a wonderful, compassionate mental health professional. The combination of these therapies, powered by prayer and the healing hand of God, gave me the strength to get well.

As part of my healing, I also learned the power of visualization. To deal with the pain I was facing, I allowed myself – albeit temporarily – to conceive in my mind what my life could look and feel like without depression. More often than not, it was a serious struggle. Oftentimes, I couldn't see it and the darkness of my depression left me stumbling around, desperate for any sliver of light and hope that I could find. Yet from time to time, when the darkness gave way to light and I experienced moments of optimism, I would try to visualize myself happy and free of sadness. If visualization puts you a little closer to seeing yourself whole again, you might consider giving it a try.

Okay, go with me on this one, just for a moment. Let's start easy. Take a deep breath. Take another one, a really deep one, one where you reach into the very depths of your soul and search for that thing that set you on the winding road of despair. Think about it. Picture it. Look at it. Don't turn away, no matter how painful it may feel. Now see yourself picking it up and putting it in a box — a very strong box that has a key, a key that only you possess. No one else has a copy or can get one. I want you to pick up that person, place or thing that set you on this course of perpetual sadness. Pick it up and put it in the box. If it feels too big, if it feels like too much, pick it up anyway. See yourself struggling with it. It's heavy and has weighed you down for far too long. It might feel like it's going to push you back to the ground or even take you out! Don't let it! Gather yourself. Gather your strength. Flatten your feet. Square your hips, bend your knees, but whatever you do, don't let go until the whole ugly thing is in the box. Box not big enough? Get a bigger one in your mind. Make it as big as you need to fit that ugly, life-sucking thing in there. Remember, once it's in there, it's not coming back out.

Are you out of breath from the weight of getting it in there? Was it heavy? Heavier than you thought? My pain was. It weighed me down for five very long years. I know how you're feeling. I understand. You're exhausted. It took all of your strength to push that thing in that box and close it shut. Now you're going to tie it, tape it, glue it, and seal it in there so that it can never come back out again.

Wow! You did it. You took the first of the many important steps you need to get your life back on track! You named the thing or person that was continuing to suck the life out of you and you faced it – at least symbolically.

Fear is another very real part of the depression experience. When we are depressed, we're also often fearful that if people find out what we're going through, they'll think we're going crazy. We're fearful that we've fallen so deeply into the shadows of life that nothing and no one can get us out. We're fearful of telling someone that we're in pain and need help. We're fearful because, for the first time in our lives, we don't know how to make things better, despite our ability to make it better for everyone else.

Okay, I need you to take another step. I want you to try to let go of your fear and your depression and let God. Huh? What do I mean by that? You need to begin to let go of the source of your depression so that you can hold onto the source of life. You've got to try to let go of being sad and in pain. You want more! I know you do. You want to see the sun again. More importantly, you want to feel the sun again — not just on the outside but deep in your soul. In the darkest days of my depression, I would see the sun shining but could never feel it. I was always cold and it was always gray, even when it was 90 degrees outside. I began to feel desperate to get better.

I know that you want to experience the joys and pleasures of life that have eluded you for so long. If you didn't, you wouldn't have bought this book. But, first, I want you to give yourself permission to accept that you may be depressed. You're not in a funk. You don't have an attitude. You are suffering from depression, and you are ready to face it and get the help that you so desperately need. I want you to let those tears flow out of you that you've kept buried deep inside. It's okay, I promise. Let go. God is here for you. He always has been and He always will be. He loves you so much and He's whispering His promise in your ear even now. "I will never leave you nor forsake you." (*Hebrews 13:5*). Pull that tissue box in a little closer and let go. It's okay to cry. It's okay to be a strong, Black Christian woman and cry. Really it is. Your tears are a gift from the Holy Spirit. They release what you cannot utter in words. Don't hold back. You know you're tired of being in this place. You're tired of looking strong but feeling weak. You're tired of feeling sad. You're tired of being tired, and angry, and empty. Cry out your pain. Cry out your sadness. Cry for the days, weeks, months and possibly even years that you've let slip by because you didn't know how to let go and let God.

I want you to take just one more step with me. Remember, I'm with you and so is God. I want you to wipe your eyes. Yes. Wipe your eyes and dry your face. Completely. Now put down the tissues in your hand. Move the tissue box from in front of you and slip it to the side. Breathe. Breathe again. Breathe slowly until you can feel your heart rate slowing down. Put your hand on your chest if you have to, but don't move forward until you can feel it slowing down. Now begin to imagine yourself releasing your pain, slowly. See yourself pushing that box down a very steep hill that empties into a very deep ocean. Once it hits the water, it will be gone forever. Allow yourself to imagine what you'll feel like without pain. Imagine how different your life can and will be. Picture yourself free of depression. Completely free. Can you see it? Feel it?

Picture what your life will look like when it is joyful. I know, for some of you, it's been a long time, a very long time. But I want you to allow your mind to go there. Imagine it! Where are you? What are you doing? Who is with you? See it! Feel it!

Go with me for just one more minute! I know it may be hard to imagine your life without depression; it's been your ever-present companion for far too long. But here's what I want you to do. I want you to imagine holding on to the side of a boat that is sailing in the middle of the ocean. The boat is moving slowly. The water is cold. It's the middle of the night. Someone is calling your name softly. You realize that you're hearing the voice of God. You almost didn't recognize it at first. You forgot what it sounded like. He's calling you. Renee, Cynthia, Andrea, Tamia, Jasmine, Keisha. He's calling your name and He's stretched out His hand toward you. He wants to lift you out of that cold, dark water. You've lost your strength. Your clothes are soaked, heavy and weighing you down. You've been holding on to the edge of the boat for what seems like forever. You're just barely hanging on but, somehow, you haven't yet let go. But what you did do is stop calling for help. You figured you'd preserve your strength by keeping quiet. Folks have passed by you in their boats not because they didn't care, but because they didn't realize you needed help. They couldn't see you. You never said a word. You had on a mask. Originally, it was to help you breathe, you know — like the kind of masks you wear when you're going scuba-diving. But, later, you used it to hide your face so that you wouldn't be seen or recognized. Fortunately, even in your hiding and in your silence, the Lord heard you.

You've been in that water for a long time and you're so close to letting go. God knows you are. You're tired of the feelings of hopelessness and despair that have taken hold of you like an anchor, pulling you down. The Lord knows that it's just a matter of time before you release your hold on the boat. You're thinking that things would be so much easier if you just let go. Then there would be no more pain, no more sadness, no more long dark days and painful, weary nights.

No! Not so! He told me to tell you that it's not time for you to let go! He knows that you're cold and tired. But wait! He's coming to get you! He's going to pull you out of that cold, dark water and place your feet on dry land. He's just a few feet away. I can see Him approaching. He's moving quickly. He knows that you're almost ready to give up. But because He knows that it's not your time yet, He speeds up. His movements are longer, swifter, more urgent. He's here! He's got your hand and He's pulling you back to safety! You forgot what it felt like to be out of the water. It's been so long. Your skin is cold and clammy and your limbs are numb. You've been in that water longer than you should have been. You're shivering and scared and maybe even confused. God wraps you in a warm, dry blanket. The blanket feels so familiar, so comforting. You're not sure why. You're disoriented, in a fog. You don't know where you are or really how you got there. Why would He pull you out now? You had accepted that your spirit would be immersed in a vast ocean of sadness and pain forever and that you'd never see the light of day again. Not so, my sistah! Not so!

The Lord has wrapped His arms around you and is speaking to you softly and tenderly. You've finally stopped shaking and shivering. He's talking to you about your life and how you got on the boat and what caused you to fall overboard. He's talking to you about the time you were sexually assaulted as a child, about losing your mother to illness, about the break-up of your marriage of 10 years. He's talking to you about Hannah and her situation. And, as He did in her time, He's telling you that your life, as you've known it, is about to change.

You're starting to feel yourself warm up, just a little. With comforting and reassuring hands, He gives you a small piece of paper. On it are some instructions. He has laid out for you the steps you need to take to get your life back on solid ground. But before you read it, you need to pray:

Lord, I thank You for pulling me out of that water. I thank You for rescuing me from the place of despair that I had come to accept as my destiny. I don't know what I've done to deserve Your mercy but I'm grateful that You chose to save me today. I've grown so used to the cold darkness of depression that has surrounded me. I'm not sure I know how to function outside of it. I'm scared. I don't know what to do or who to talk to, but I know You are with me. Thank You for saving me. Thank You for this warm blanket. Thank You for Your reassuring voice. Thank You for pulling me out of that vast ocean of despair. Now please guide me as I try to figure out what to do next. In Jesus' name I pray. Amen.

Chapter 5
Lay Down The Masks,
Lay Them Down!

We wear the mask that grins and lies,
It hides our cheeks and shades our eyes, —
This debt we pay to human guile;
With torn and bleeding hearts we smile,
And mouth with myriad subtleties.

Why should the world be over-wise,
In counting all our tears and sighs?
Nay, let them only see us, while
We wear the mask.

We smile but, O great Christ, our cries
To thee from tortured souls arise.
We sing, but oh the clay is vile
Beneath our feet, and long the mile;

But let the world dream otherwise,
We wear the mask!

Paul Laurence Dunbar

Y ou're out of the water. You've dried off. Your body tem-
perature is slowly coming back to normal. You look
down at the piece of paper that the Lord placed in your hands.
It says: *"I'm calling you to a place of restoration. I want you to*
follow these steps as part of your journey out of depression to a place
of mental, emotional and spiritual healing."

But wait! You're still carrying something that you need to
get rid of in order to get to that place of peace. It's that mask!
You put it on such a long time ago and forgot you still had
it on. Over time, you've collected so many masks that now
you've got one for everywhere you go and for every day of the
week. You have the mask that you wear at work. You know,
that successful, accomplished, never-gonna-let-you-see-me-
sweat mask. And then there's the mask that you wear around
your family. That's the one that says go-to person across your
forehead, the one folks come to when they need to vent, or
cry or just borrow a few bucks till payday. And, of course, we
can't forget the mask you wear at church. That's the one that
you wear when you serve on the trustee or usher board, help
with the youth ministry, or lead praise and worship at the 8,

61

10 and noontime services! And, finally, there's the mask that you've been wearing to fool yourself! That's the mask that you wear at home. You know, the one that you wear to tell yourself that everything is okay when you really know that it isn't. It's time for healing. It's time to lay down the masks, girl. Lay them down!

Masks come in every size, shape and color! Their purpose is to disguise, conceal and protect your face. They hide your identity; they hide who you really are. Under your mask may lie a beautiful, sensitive, caring woman who may have been injured or scarred beyond recognition by the trials of life. Under your mask may lie a woman full of passion and energy whose spirit has been broken and whose zeal for life sucked dry. Under your mask may lie a mother, a daughter, a sister or a friend who, while still physically present, is emotionally somewhere very far away. You may have been using your many masks to hide your face and your pain. I don't blame you for that. I understand. Your masks have become your most reliable form of protection. Protection from the pain, from those who would see your hurt and not know how to deal with it, and from those circumstances that led you down this dark path of depression. If you are anything like me, you wore your mask for so long that going without it made you feel exposed and vulnerable. But it gets hot under there. You can't breathe. You can't relax. You can't be yourself when you wear a mask.

When we're depressed, we often try to disguise or conceal our pain with expensive make-up and makeovers. We figure that even if we feel rotten on the inside, we should at least look fabulous on the outside! So we buy our MAC, Revlon, our Flori Roberts and our Ebony Fashion Fair by the truck-load. We spend hundreds and sometimes thousands of dollars on our hair — going from short to long, black to blond, permed to natural, braids to weaves, all in an attempt to look better! I was guilty. I won't even try to pretend that I didn't hide myself during my long stint with depression. I figured if I looked good, I wouldn't feel bad. Can I get a witness? The truth is, no matter how good we may look on the outside, if we haven't effectively addressed our depression, all that stuff – the hair, the make-up, and the clothes – is just treating the surface, not our spirits.

I'm sure you're familiar with the term "functional alcoholic." This is a person who meets the criteria for a medical diagnosis for alcohol dependence but who is highly functional in society. The functional alcoholic still has a job, can maintain a home and very often has active connections to family. This individual rarely misses work and other obligations because of drinking and usually excels at work and career. Very often, a functional alcoholic is a clever and perhaps even engaging individual who is successful in many areas of life. To all but those who are closest to the functional alcoholic, this individual gives the *outward* appearance of being perfectly normal.

I believe that many Black women live as functionally depressed women. We go to church and work and school, week after week, month after month, and sometimes even year after year, giving the appearance of being okay, minus the occasional funk or attitude. To all who look at us, we appear to be happy, healthy, vibrant and successful leaders, colleagues, family members, and fellow church members. And for those of us who have achieved a certain degree of success or visibility in our careers, churches and communities and are still struggling with depression, God help us. Many times, our very success creates even more pressure to hide behind our careers and our clothes and our cars, causing us not to want anyone to know what's really going on inside us. The truth is, so many of us are hurting and in pain.

In my own experience, having won the respect of my colleagues and peers, the growing attention of my clients, and the expectation that I would take a strong leadership role in our church's music ministry — all of these achievements created an overwhelming amount of pressure to keep up appearances. And as so many Black women do, I took on more and more, telling myself that I could handle it all when, in reality, my depression sucked more and more life out of me every day. I pulled my mask tighter and tighter with each passing year of my depression, hoping that no one would see my downward spiral. What's even more sad: It worked.

One of the biggest problems with wearing a mask is that it hides not only you from people but also people from you. It also makes it very hard to talk. And so, you don't. You keep your best mask on, whip your hair into shape — Lord knows, we won't go anywhere if our hair isn't right — put your best outfit on and walk out the door with your head held high or at least *looking* like you're holding your head high.

As strong Black women, we've been conditioned not to name our pain. And, more specifically, we don't give a name to our depression. We call it everything else but what it is. We tell ourselves and each other that "we're too blessed to be stressed" and keep on rolling. Well, that's okay as a slogan on a t-shirt. But the truth is, more often than not, we are too stressed to be blessed! Our depression, our pain, and our many masks block not only our ability to realize fully the blessings of God but also our ability to acknowledge what's happening inside.

At first, that's what I did. I wore my Ms. Corporate America mask every day from 9 am to 5 pm. From 5 to 6 pm, I would, like Hannah be "in bitterness of soul," and would weep non-stop from the time I put my key in the ignition of my car until the time I turned into my long, winding driveway in the suburbs. I had programmed myself to change masks, to start wiping my tears and getting my face together, by about 5:45 pm. That way, by the time I got home, no one was the wiser. I mastered the art of hiding my true emotions and I was even more vigilant about hiding my pain. From 6 to 10 p.m., I would wear my mommy, wife and friend mask. From 10 p.m. to 2 a.m., I would put on my consummate entrepreneur mask, working to get my consulting practice off the ground. From 2 to 7 a.m., I would lay down my many masks and toss back and forth in my bed, carrying the stresses of the days and weeks gone by like a bad habit, never really able to quite shake them loose. I did that five days a week for almost five years. On the outside, I looked like Superwoman. But, on the inside, I was an absolute mess and nobody knew it. Absolutely nobody.

I know you're thinking to yourself: Well, that was a crazy schedule! No wonder she was depressed! She drove herself into the ground. To that, I would reply, you're absolutely right. I didn't get enough rest. I didn't eat properly. I didn't make quality time for myself or my family. I didn't even make enough time for God. I had none of the balance needed to be a healthy, happy woman, wife, mother, sister or friend. My depression affected so many more people than just myself. Yours does too. But of course, I didn't realize that at the time. If I only had the wisdom and understanding then that I do now. Hindsight is indeed 20-20.

Looking back on my life, I recognize how many things were wrong with that pattern: 1) I not only fooled others, but I tried to fool myself into believing that everything was alright. Why do we do that? Why have we bought into this strong, Black woman myth? It's killing so many of us! 2) I accepted my perpetual feelings of sadness and despair as normal. We all get the blues sometimes, right? 3) I spoke to no one about how I was feeling. Instead, I locked myself in my own prison of silence and threw away the key; and, 4) I was slowly killing myself – emotionally, mentally, physically and most important, spiritually — one painful day at a time.

Spiritual death probably was one of the most frightening experiences of my life. I say frightening because the idea of permanently losing my connection with God put me in an even more isolated place. I knew that I could not exist without the presence of God in my life while, at the same time, I felt distanced from Him. I was embarrassed and ashamed that as a God-fearing, Bible-reading, church-going, praise team-leading Christian, I couldn't get control over my depression! What kind of Christian, what kind of strong Black woman was I, to be messed up this badly? Negative self-talk comes so naturally when we are depressed. In depression, we get so used to negativity that we often reinforce our worst beliefs about ourselves, which in turn makes us feel worse. Instead of hearing the positive, reassuring words of God and others, we become silent and we talk to no one. We wear our masks and ignore our pain, when in reality we are enduring deep, profound sadness. That's the part of my story that you've got to understand. I suspect that it's an important part of your story, too.

Let me illustrate the craziness of silence in depression. Imagine you are carrying a baby. Nine months have gone by, and it's time to go to the hospital for the delivery. The bags are packed. The doctor's been called, and the support team is standing by. You arrive at the labor and delivery department of the hospital and are met by a team of nurses ready to usher you through the delivery process. You have been carrying this precious life for nine months. That's a long time! Now it's time for a new life to emerge. But instead of lying down in a quiet, soothing room and getting into a posture to deliver, you decide to go home. You're afraid. You've never had a baby before. You don't know what's going to happen once this child is born. And so, without saying a word, you and your big belly get up and walk out. Now remember, the baby is ready to enter this world. And while it's warm and cozy inside your womb, your little bundle of joy has run out of room in there and wants to look into the eyes of the voice she has been hearing for the last nine months.

Everyone is confused. It's time to have the baby! Where are you going? The nurses try to encourage you to lie back down.

The doctor is on her way. You say nothing. You're afraid, but you don't want anyone to know it. You don't know how to tell them that you're afraid to be a mother. There's confusion all around you. No one understands what's going. Everyone can clearly see that you're pregnant, ready-to-deliver pregnant, but you're walking out of the hospital.

If you would just say something — tell your girlfriend, your mother, the nurses what is going on — they could help you. They could call in all the resources available to help you through your fears and assure you that you will have a safe and healthy delivery. But still you say nothing. Your baby is starting to push her way out. "Let me out, Mommy. I can't wait to see you!" she says. But instead you force yourself toward the door. Your fear of delivering and motherhood and all the other unknowns before you and your child have paralyzed you into silence. You walk out of the hospital doors, hail the nearest cab and pull off, leaving everyone on the curb scratching their heads in amazement and concern for your safety.

The cab driver looks in his rearview mirror at you. He's sees you're in distress, but he says nothing. Instead, he asks you where you want to go. You don't know. You say nothing. He waits. The meter is running. You say nothing. He shifts impatiently in his seat, waiting for you to give instructions about where he should take you. But at this point you're really afraid. You feel trapped in this dingy, dirty cab. You've left the hospital, and those who would have taken care of you. You don't know where you're going or even why! Crazy? Yes, it is.

This little story illustrates what happens to us when we suffer depression in silence. We do irrational things. We put our physical, mental, emotional and spiritual health at risk. Not intentionally most times, but we do. And, despite having a team of folks at our disposal to help us through our pain and confusion, we say nothing. We're confused, and sometimes those closest to us are, too. They don't understand our change in behavior or our silence. They can't make sense of the changes they see in us. We look one way but really feel something completely different.

This is not the way to go. We have to open our mouths and speak! Ask for help! Tell someone we trust that we're afraid and don't know what to do. It's okay. Really it is.

I want to encourage you, right now, to seek God for the confidence that you need to reach out to someone – anyone –about your depression. Know that it's going to be okay. But first, let's pray:

Dear God: I stand in the gap for my sister who is coming face to face with her pain, anguish and fear of facing her depression. She's tired of wearing her game-face. Her many masks are breaking down, and she's desperate to re-emerge from the shadows where she has lived far too long. Lord, I need You to cover her with Your Holy

Spirit. Stand up in her even now, oh God. Plant a seed in her heart and mind that will allow her to see herself strong and whole again. Give her strength from the inside and let Your grace shine on the outside, God, as only You can. Give her the spirit of determination that will drive her to seek the help that she so desperately needs. I believe in the power of Your spirit and Your ability to do anything but fail. In Jesus' name. Amen.

Chapter 6
You Gotta Talk!

In my distress I called to the LORD;
I cried to my God for help.
From his temple he heard my voice;
my cry came before him, into his ears.

Psalms 18:6 (NIV)

Growing up, I had the benefit of being in a family that treated talking as a sport! Funny, none of us were heavily into real sports, but talking — we did that well. It seemed that we talked often and openly about everything from relationships to church to politics to race. Talking, like a good game of chess, was something to be refined, perfected, and mastered. Even as children, we were encouraged to share our opinions. We learned to make our points and stand our ground. We argued and debated loudly and with passion. We laughed, cried and spoke with conviction and pride. Doing so was like a rite of passage and made us true Browns and Mattocks (my mother's maiden name). I loved the freedom and sense of empowerment that I felt during those early kitchen-table discussions. It was through those childhood and adolescent experiences that I learned the importance of talking.

If they awarded degrees in talking about one's feelings, I probably would have graduated with honors! Not only did I master the art of talking, or so I thought, but I also learned the importance of letting myself cry. Our much celebrated family gatherings often included tears. We cried when we were happy. We cried when we were angry. And of course, we cried when we were sad. I was conditioned to let my emotions show pretty freely. Being stoic and unemotional was not part of the Brown-Mattock bloodline — quite the opposite, actually. We often were confounded by people who were closed, intensely private, and not open with their emotions. Ironic, isn't it?

Now I recognize that my experience may be a little different from yours. Talking is in my DNA, and I'm glad for it. But I know that every family doesn't communicate at the same level as mine. In many families, talking openly about feelings and emotions is absolutely taboo. Regardless of which side of the talking fence you grew up on, it's important to understand the value and freedom that you can experience by talking through your pain.

Please don't misunderstand me here. As the old folks say, "Everything ain't for everybody." I realize that we sometimes have to be careful about what we talk about and with whom. There are some conversations that are appropriate for immediate family members and close friends, and there are others that are appropriate for colleagues and acquaintances. More importantly, there are other conversations that should be had only with the Lord. The key is knowing whom to talk to and when. Of course, only you can decide that. That said, not talking at all is almost never the best option!

We don't know much about Hannah's life but I'm going to make an educated guess that she didn't grow up sharing her feelings openly and freely. You may have grown up the same way. Or, like me, you may have inherited the gift of gab and come from a long line of talkers. This is not about who had a better upbringing or even about who learned to talk more. It's about keeping silent when you need to talk. That's what Hannah did. When things got really bad, when the pain and stress of not being able to conceive became too much for her, she kept silent. She internalized her pain.

You would think that, given my bent toward talking, that I would have freely shared my thoughts and feelings with my closest family and friends when I was going through my own

Hannah experience. Well it didn't. I not only became silent about my depression but, like Hannah, I stifled my own pain so much so that it prolonged my bout of depression.

Why? Why would someone from an open, loving, supportive Christian family like mine not talk when she was going through a difficult time? I could give a million reasons. I think one of the most compelling was my effort to live up to the role I had assumed in my family. I was the one everybody thought was opinionated, strong, and had it all together. And so, how could I let them down, right? How could I shatter the image they had of me? How could I disappoint them and let them see that I really didn't have it all together like they thought I did? And so, rather than disappoint those I cared about the most, I turned my pain inward in an attempt to spare those I loved.

The Bible is not specific about how many years Hannah lived in despair. If I Samuel 1:7 is any indication, it was many years. Sis, let me tell you something. There's a time to speak, and there's a time to remain silent. Staying silent while you are depressed is a recipe for disaster! Please understand that! Pain that is silenced only brings slow death – emotional death, mental death, spiritual death, and sometimes even physical death. Yes, long-term sadness and pain, not properly dealt with, can and will kill you and your spirit. The worse part is that it will kill your mind first, and then attack your body. Ah, but God sent me to tell you that it's not your time to die! You shall not die but live! *(Psalms 118: 17, NIV)* And, despite your current situation, your test is about to be your testimony!

Even though I've always considered myself a talker, I could never find the words to tell anyone what I was going through. Not my sisters, not my mother, not my husband, no one. I realize now that I was not unique in my silence. So many of us remain silent in and about our depression. We are silent for a myriad of reasons. Sometimes we're silent because we don't want people in our business. Sometimes we're silent because our pain is so profound, so intense that we can't put it into words. Sometimes we're silent because we believe that if we just ignore our feelings, they'll go away with time. In reality, we merely defer the process of facing that person, place or thing that brought us here.

As part of my research for this book, I wanted to better understand this tendency. It is said that silence is the glue that holds depression within us. It is silence – the withholding, repression, denial, and isolation — that leads to overwhelming sadness, disinterest, fatigue, chronic pain and all manner of acting out in socially inappropriate ways. And unfortunately, that same silence seems to affect us so much more than our White sisters. Somehow they seem more comfortable talking about getting help for their depression; they consider them-selves more entitled. I especially wanted to understand if my experience of enduring depression silently was different from the experiences of other Black women. And so, I sought out some of the nation's most prominent, most respected psychologists, nurses, authors and businesswomen to learn about their experiences treating sistahs or living with depression themselves.

One of my most memorable conversations was with businesswoman and author Terrie Williams. Terrie is a clinical social worker by training who became a highly successful public relations mogul later in her professional life. Her most recent book, *Black Pain: It Just Looks Like We're Not Hurting*, is one of the most up-to-date and comprehensive books about depression within the Black community.

She's got a fiercely busy schedule, but she consented to speak with me as I was writing this book. Terrie, a sufferer of chronic and crippling depression herself and now a staunch advocate for depression awareness and prevention, talked with me about this silence phenomenon. "We need to be gentle with ourselves. We've passed our pain from generation to generation, and so one of our biggest challenges is that we're not familiar with speaking about it. Talking and seeking professional help [for our depression] is foreign to us."

Terrie has found a way to shatter the walls of silence that we've built around this thing called depression. In *Black Pain*, she speaks openly about her own depression. "When women see that I'm living through my pain, talking about it openly and without shame, they believe that maybe, just maybe, it's possible for them to do the same. Talking about my pain isn't the hardest part anymore; it's trying to get the women I meet to understand that the beginning of a way to heal our pain lies in our willingness to look at the issues that make up its foundation."

Of course, it's particularly hard to talk about your depression if you don't really know what it is or can't give it a name. I also had the privilege of speaking with Dr. Freda Lewis Hall, former practicing psychologist and now senior vice president and chief medical officer with Pfizer Inc. Before her work in the pharmaceutical industry, Dr. Lewis-Hall practiced psychology at Howard University Hospital in Washington, D.C. There her client base largely consisted of women of color whom she described as "never having any cracks in their armor." These women often "shared a long history of overcoming, making it difficult for them to recognize the pressures and stressors of life that triggered their depression." And then, even after realizing that they had a problem with prolonged periods of sadness, many of these women failed to seek professional help for as many as 10 years.

She spoke of women whom she had treated who told her "they didn't know what their depression was." In the Black community, "we often don't give depression a name. We attribute our symptoms to other events, conditions and situations. And, like everything else, we think that our sadness will pass just like the many changing events in our lives." If we just wait it out, keep working through and around it, it will go away.

According to Dr. Lewis-Hall, the widespread belief that depression is experienced only by rich White women is simply wrong. "Depression is an equal opportunity illness," she said. "It's not a cultural condition. And despite the 'cultural wraps' we put around it, depression continues to be cloaked in our culture. We really need to de-stigmatize it. We are more likely to be hit by depression than we are to be hit by a car! And the faster we are able to recognize it, talk about it, and treat it, the better."

She added that "the key to depression is recognizing that it's not your fault. It doesn't come as a result of something you did wrong. If you look at it that way, and are willing to talk about it, then seeking treatment becomes a little easier."

We gotta talk about what's happening to us. Our silence is killing us. It's taking away our ability to build even stronger families and businesses and legacies that could be passed on to our children's children.

I finally realized that not talking about my depression was killing me. Literally! It took me a long time to get there though — a very long time. It's taken me even longer to talk openly about my experience. More than 10 years, to be exact.

I never dreamed that I could put pen to paper and describe a mental health condition that almost ruined my life. But now — much like Terrie Williams, who has committed much of her time and resources to addressing depression in the Black community — I refuse to be silent!

I really want you to break your silence. I strongly believe that talking about what's happening within you will make the difference between life and emotional, mental, spiritual and even physical death. Open your mouth and let the burdens of your spirit come pouring out of you. They are weighing you down and probably have been for a very long time. You gotta get free! You gotta talk! But first, let's pray:

Dear Lord, we come before You now because our minds are messed up. We've held on to our pain for far too long. We have embraced a silence that is now killing us. We're afraid and don't know what to do. But we know that if we just ask, You will heal and restore not only our minds, but also our bodies and spirits, to a place of peace. Oh God, we come to You now because we know that You are able. Please forgive us for not talking to You before. We didn't know what to say or how to express our pain. But now, Lord, we are ready to be delivered from the burdens of sadness and despair that have taken over our lives. We're ready to talk to You and to those who can help us be the women You have called us to be. Please guide us and direct us to those we can trust to help us out of this valley of depression. We're standing on Your promises, Lord. In Jesus' name we pray. Amen.

Chapter 7

So Who Are You Talking To?

~:❀:~

> *The road to emotional freedom*
> *is often paved with tears and words.*
> *Words of absolute truth.*

> *Me*

For the sake of your health, you must find someone you can talk to. Your life depends on it! You've read, cried, prayed and now you're beginning to feel a sense of renewed hope that you can experience life after depression.

So now comes the challenging part; you know you need to talk but you don't know who to talk to. When do you start talking? Where do you go? What do you say? First, talk to God. I will warn you, though that it may feel as if God isn't hearing you and you're not hearing Him. You may even tell yourself that prayer is a waste of time because nothing is going to make a difference in your sad, dark life. That's the devil, and he's a liar!

James 5:16 tells us that "the effectual fervent prayer of a righteous man (or woman) availeth much!" Talk to God. He will hear and answer you. Get yourself in a quiet place. Away from the things, people and circumstances that are weighing you down. Start small. Do it for just one hour. Get to that place that will allow you to quiet the doubt and fear in your mind, and call out to God like you never have before. It's normal to feel fear and doubt at first. As hard as it may be, don't judge yourself. Just try to let go long enough to talk to God and for Him to talk to you. He's waiting to hear from you, and you desperately need to hear from Him. God and prayer are two of your most important weapons for combating your depression.

Let's go back to Hannah for a moment. Her story gives us a wonderful lesson about the power of prayer. Hannah was desperate for relief from the pain and despair she was experiencing. Don't miss this! She was absolutely desperate! Much like you probably are now. She knew she couldn't continue living in silence, internalizing her sorrow and the emptiness that came as a result of her infertility. And so, she let go of any posturing and pretense that she may have had and poured her guts out to God. Hannah's prayer wasn't some polite, poised petition, but one in which she completely emptied herself of every burden that was weighing her down. Look at I Samuel 1:15. In Biblical terms, the term "pouring out" normally is associated with the pouring of liquids, particularly blood and water in connection with sacrifices. In some Old Testament passages, the term also is used in connection with prayer. When you "pour" yourself out to God, you're being absolutely honest with Him, expressing your deepest pain and fears. And when you do, says Terrie Williams, when you pray about your depression, "God will go to the deepest, darkest, most shameful place with you." He won't leave you. He won't judge you. He won't forsake you!

Hannah was so absorbed in her prayer and pleading to God that she became oblivious to those around her and to what they might think of her. I need you to get there! I need you to not care what folk think or say about you! This moment, right here, isn't about them. It's about you and getting your life back. Do this for you! Do it as if your very life depends on it! It does!

Before Hannah spoke to anyone else, she knew that she needed talk to the Lord. Please do not misunderstand what I'm saying here. I am not at all suggesting that a support group or a structured therapy program or regular meetings with a mental health professional are a waste of time. Quite the contrary! Your treatment can and should include a combination of therapy and prayer and also may include medication. But you must start with the One who can do anything but fail, the One who will bring you a peace that passes all understanding! That One is God.

That said, I completely agree with Sylvia Lackey, staff therapist at the Family Institute at Northwestern University and a licensed clinical social worker. An expert on depression, Sylvia spoke at the Second Annual Conference on Depression sponsored in 2007 by the Mt. Zion Apostolic Tabernacle Church in Evanston, Illinois. At that conference, she spoke about her strong belief in prayer. But she also spoke about her concern that some Christians berate those who have depression, suggesting that sufferers of depression must not really believe in God if they seek the counsel of a therapist or take medication. God gives us the wisdom and ability to pray. He also gives us the wisdom to seek professional help when we need it. The two things are not mutually exclusive and can and should co-exist.

Sylvia went on to talk about what she's heard and experienced as a woman of faith herself. I'm sure that, if you've been in church long enough, you've heard someone say, "Girl, all you have to do is pray and Jesus will work it out." Or maybe you've heard one of the church mothers say, "Let me get that oil and anoint you and rebuke that spirit in the name of Jesus." Don't get me wrong, there were times during my years of depression that I wished someone would have poured a whole bottle of blessed oil on my head. But being a Christian woman who seeks the help of God and a mental health professional is not an either-or proposition but a yes-and one! There is power in prayer and value in seeking professional help. Make no mistake about it. As Sylvia stated in her important conference presentation, "Your faith tradition, whatever it may be, does not — I repeat, does not — have to compete with the care provided by a mental health professional." If you broke your foot, you would go to the podiatrist. If you were suffering from heart disease, you would go to see a cardiologist. Why not also take care of your mind by seeking help from someone who is trained to do so? I can't emphasize this enough.

One of our other biggest challenges as women of faith is that we don't talk about mental health problems in the church. Like issues of rape, incest, molestation and family dysfunction, mental illness is not a condition that most of us are comfortable talking about. We've been conditioned to keep our business to ourselves, pray and let God do the rest. But chances are the person whose hand you held while praying during last week's service is suffering from or has suffered from some form of mental illness — or knows someone who has. You have to know that you're not alone. The interesting thing is that, according to Dr. Lewis-Hall, "Once educated, the church can be an ardent supporter for seeking treatment. Church can provide strength when we need it." Our churches and pastors can be important partners when seeking treatment.

In addition to talking to God, I also strongly encourage you to actively seek out the support of your pastor or another man or woman of God concerning your situation. You can't live out your spiritual purpose if you are living in a state of depression. Let me say that again: You can't live out your spiritual purpose if you are living in a state of depression. It's almost impossible to be the wife, mother, sister, daughter or friend that God has called you to be when your way is dark with perpetual sadness and despair.

Many times our pastors and ministers are available to us as a resource, waiting for us to call, and we don't say a word. We sit in silence out of fear, shame or embarrassment, especially when we have a position of prominence in the church. We don't want anyone, including the pastor, to know about our situation when we ourselves are expected to minister and encourage others. We have to let that go, my sistahs! Church folk got problems, too! We experience many of the same challenges as people outside of the church. Being members of the body of Christ does not exempt us from sometimes needing and seeking the expertise of professionals who can help us!

Whether you choose to talk only to God, or also to your pastor and a therapist is ultimately your decision. Whatever you do, I encourage you, like Hannah, to speak to God first.

He will guide you according to His plan for your recovery and will put the right people in your path at the right time for you to consult with. That doesn't mean that you should be undiscerning about whom you choose to talk to about your situation. Be selective and strategic. Seek out the counsel of those spiritual leaders and professionals who have demonstrated a commitment to keeping your best interests at heart.

A word of caution, and please take this in the spirit in which it is intended — one of encouragement and not of criticism. If you know that your pastor is a wonderful preacher or teacher but may not have the gift of compassion or the skills to counsel you through your situation, seek out someone else on your church's ministerial staff whom you can trust. Partnering with the right spiritual leader at this point in your recovery is critical to your healing.

That said, you must remember that pastors are people too. They have their own challenges and issues and sometimes they are not in a good place – mentally or emotionally – to guide you through your situation. In her book, *Black Pain*, Terrie Williams relates a conversation about this issue with Obery Hendricks. Dr. Hendricks is Professor of Biblical Interpretation at New York Theological Seminary and past president of Payne Theological Seminary, the oldest African American seminary in the nation. He says, "Many of our churches are not really equipped to make a difference [for depressed people in the congregation] because there's no real tradition for looking deep inside yourself, or meditation, contemplation and introspection." There is a strong possibility that your pastor might be a wonderful leader but not a good counselor. Or the extent of your depression goes beyond his or her ability to provide help. Terrie speaks about this dynamic very candidly. There is sometimes an unfair expectation that pastors can give more comfort than they can. "Their own insecurities as human beings make them hesitate to steer us to mental health professionals, even though that's what we really need."

And so, if you reach out to your pastor but you don't feel confident about his or her ability to support you during this critical point in your life, then reach out beyond your congregation. Ask a friend who is a part of a God-focused, Spirit-led ministry, and see if you can get the help that you need there. Our pastors and churches are just one of the places we should seek assistance, not the only place.

In addition to getting spiritual guidance and support, I also strongly encourage you talk to a qualified mental health professional. Many of us have this thing about speaking to psychologists or therapists. We don't want folks to think we're crazy or get in our business. Some of us have even been raised not to trust people outside of our families, when it comes to personal, private matters. Or sometimes, we go into therapy with one foot in the door and one foot out. In the interests of your mental, emotional and spiritual restoration and recovery, please let that go! There are many highly qualified mental health professionals to guide you out of your depression in a respectful and confidential way. Seek out someone who has experience treating this condition and get back on the road that God has assigned you to travel. The road called "depression" is not it!

According to Dr. Lewis-Hall, "we are skittish [about going to therapy] and we often wonder if we're making something out of nothing. We come into therapy needing validation that our feelings are real." To that I say if you feel it, then it's real to you! Don't ignore your pain.

Start by consulting your employer's health plan or employee assistance plan (EAP). Most employer-provided health plans include some sort of mental health coverage and often also include EAP services. An EAP is a confidential employee benefit, typically offered by employers free of charge or a very little cost that helps employees deal with personal problems that might adversely impact their work performance, health, and well-being. Services include substance abuse assistance, bereavement and marital counseling, help with weight issues, and referrals to wellness resources including those helpful in the struggle against depression. EAP services are usually provided by a third-party, rather than the employer itself, and the company receives only summary statistical data from the service provider. Employees' names and services received are kept confidential. Check with your healthcare provider or human resources representative for guidance.

There also are likely to be social service agencies in your area that offer affordable or free counseling. Check with your local nonprofit community health organization to see what may be available. If money is less of a concern, I encourage you to find a qualified therapist in private practice. Interview that person first to ensure compatibility with your communication style and an understanding of the kinds of cultural issues that may contribute to your current condition. If, after the first two or three sessions, you don't feel comfortable, find someone else. Your relationship with your therapist is not a marriage; it does not have to be a life-long commitment. If it's no longer working for you or it feels as if it's not helping you reach your goal of optimum mental health, move on. Whatever you do, don't give up on finding someone you can trust and feel comfortable with. To find a psychologist or therapist near you, check out the American Psychological Association. It offers a free, searchable list of their member psychologists by Zip code.

When seeking out a therapist, you should be mindful of the issue of cultural competence. Cultural competence involves the use of sensitivity when interacting with other cultures and the ability to "engage meaningfully in interactions with persons from different cultural experiences." According to Dr. Barbara Jones Warren, when a professional is culturally competent, "they acknowledge and understand African American women's cultural strengths and values so that they can counsel them effectively." This doesn't mean your counselor or therapist has to be an African American or even a person of color. What it does mean is that your life experiences as a Black woman impacts your perspective and life views. Working with a professional who can be sensitive to that perspective is a key step to realizing effective treatment.

Let's go back to the Bible for a moment. Let's look at I Samuel 1:10 again. It tells us three key things: 1) Hannah was in bitterness of soul; 2) she prayed unto the Lord; and 3) she wept sore. Notice that even after she prayed, she cried. That's what you may experience too. You know you are depressed. You've cried. You've prayed and sought the Lord. You've cried some more. I'm hoping that at this point you may have even gone a step farther and sought the guidance of a professional counselor or therapist. If you have, I applaud you for that. I really do. We as Black women think we can handle everything and, as long as we've got Mama and "our girls," we're alright. I hate to say it, but sometimes Mama and the girls are part of the problem. God knows, I love my mother and my sis-

Chapter 8
Healing

~:❀:~

There's healing for your sorrow

Healing for your pain

Healing for your spirit

There's shelter from the rain

Lord send the healing

For this we know

There is a balm in Gilead

For there's a balm in Gilead

There is a balm in Gilead

To heal the soul.

Richard Smallwood

Gospel Artist & Composer

Hannah knew that if she could just get some time alone with God, away from the family-reunion activities and the provoking, irritating taunts of Penninah, God would give her the peace she was seeking.

She was weary, wounded – at least, emotionally – and sad. She was tired of the persistent feelings of emptiness that surrounded and lived within her. In an attempt to seek relief from her pain and despair, she made a simple yet heartfelt promise to God. In I Samuel 1:11 (KJV), she prayed: "If you look on my affliction and remember me, and not forget me but will give me a son, I will give him unto you all the days of my life."

You'll notice that at the point that Hannah became most desperate, she got very specific with God. Not only did she ask the Lord for a son, she also promised to never cut his hair as a symbol of her gratitude. She told God exactly what she needed from Him and exactly what she would do in return.

Despite your depression, despite how long you've carried the burden of sadness, despite how strong a Black woman you are, I want you to get very specific with God. Tell Him exactly what you need from Him. Whether it's peace of mind, a restored sense of self-esteem, the ability to forgive those who may have hurt you, or simply faith that you will be healed of your depression, tell God what you want.

During the darkest days of my depression, my husband and I went on a Caribbean cruise for our 10th wedding anniversary. It was supposed to be a wonderful trip. Deep down inside, I had hoped for a time of rest, rejuvenation, and great weather. I went shopping, loaded up on a few new outfits, got my hair done, and was ready to set sail.

Instead, because I hadn't yet dropped my got-it-all-together façade, I went on what was supposed to be a wonderful trip hurting and in pain. For four days of the cruise, I pretended to have a great time. I laughed and smiled with my husband and the other guests on the ship, participated in many of the onboard activities, and took daily excursions ashore. Here we were in the middle of the Atlantic Ocean, riding the waves on a giant cruise ship with all the food and fun you could stand, and I was miserable. Anybody been there?

If you are anything like I was during my depression, you could be surrounded by the things and people that should make you happy and, instead, you feel sad, despondent and unable to shake that haunting sense of emptiness. That, my sistahs, is depression. It's not being in a funk. It's not the blues. The blues may last a day or two, three at the most. Depression, or "bitterness of soul" as the Bible refers to it, is real. Most importantly, if left untreated, it can become debilitating. But you know that already.

I know I don't need to tell you that, in depression, everything looks gray. No matter how bright the sun might be shining in the sky, when you're depressed, you feel anguish and despair. Rarely a day passes without your crying. And your tears often have very little to do with what is happening around you and everything with what you're feeling inside. Like quicksand, you feel yourself being sucked in and your own best personal efforts won't set you free. For me, my five years of depression were the darkest, most suffocating years of my entire life. Many times I felt I couldn't breathe under the weight of my pain.

But, like Hannah, I finally got tired of my situation. I knew there had to be more for me than this sad, miserable existence. As a child of God, I knew that the Lord didn't want me to live this way. God so wants us to prosper and be in good health! You've got to believe that!

On the very last day of the cruise, my husband and I went our separate ways — he went swimming in one of those gigantic on-deck pools, and I, a non-swimmer, sat in a lounge chair on the top deck of the ship.

I found a quiet spot, shut out the world and, for what seemed like hours, I stared out at the water, waves tossing high, and pleaded with God to give me my life back. I was tired of wearing my many masks when inside all I felt was pain and sadness. I was tired of pretending to be okay when I wasn't. I was tired of the mental, emotional and physical fatigue that had slowly sucked every ounce of life out of me. I missed feeling joy, peace and happiness. I wanted to feel normal again.

I heard the voice of God that day more clearly that at any other time in my life. He spoke to me through the clouds and the sun and the lapping of the ocean's waves. We – God and I – talked for hours that day. Much like Hannah, I poured out my soul and the pain and anguish I had been carrying around for five long years. I talked to Him about everything. I took off my many masks and tossed them into the deep, blue sea. I told God everything I couldn't tell my husband, my mother, my sisters, and my best friends. He listened without judgment or blame and assured me that everything would be alright. No one understands like God. Really.

After pouring out my soul to God that afternoon on the ocean, I could, for what felt like the first time in a very long time, really feel the sun shining. I could feel the warmth of its rays on my skin, enveloping me in a place of calm and safety. God's peace covered me like a warm, thick blanket on a cold winter's day, and comforted me from the inside out.

I knew that day I had received my breakthrough.

I promised the Lord, that if He would just deliver me from this depression, if He would just give me my life back, I would serve Him with everything I had. If He would just give me back some joy, I would honor him with my life and be a living testimony to His goodness and kindness. I promised to share my story. It has taken me over 10 years to get to the point of being comfortable enough to share my testimony; I owe it to the Lord to tell of His goodness.

I pray that when you get to the point in your depression that you just can't take the sadness and despair anymore, you'll find yourself with a newfound drive and determination to get your life back. And when you do, know that everyone around you may not understand. They've become used to your sadness and anger and emotional absence. That's okay. They're about to see a new you! And now that you have some tools in your arsenal and you've given yourself permission to face your depression, you're going to get the help that you need. You're coming back better than ever! Remember, though, no matter what, you're doing this for you, not for anyone else.

Sometimes as you claw your way out of the valley of depression, people – family, friends and co-workers – may look at you like you've lost your mind. But once you've decided that you've had absolutely enough, with the help of God, a qualified mental health professional, and the support of those who love you, you will find the strength to turn depression on its head and run it out of your life for good! Let everyone think you're crazy for while. That's okay. You're on a mission to get your life back! Folks will catch on after a while! Trust me.

Let's go back to the story of Hannah one final time. So Eli, watching her pray with earnestness and desperation, thinks that Hannah has had a few too many at the family get-together and admonishes her to put away her wine. She assures him that she's had no strong drink, but that she's simply pouring out her soul to the Lord. As part of your healing, you've got to pour out your soul before the Lord! Empty yourself of your weariness and fatigue. Tell God that you desperately want and need your life back so that you can worship Him and fulfill His purpose for your life. I promise you, He has a purpose just for you. And as He did for Hannah, the Lord will hear and answer your cry.

Pay attention to Hannah and how she communicated with Eli. You'll notice that at no time did she go into any details with him about her situation. Interestingly, his role at that moment was not that of therapist or counselor. His purpose in Hannah's life at that moment in time was simply to confirm what God had already told her. And Hannah knew because she herself had already spoken with God. Eli's advice to Hannah was simple. He said: "Go in peace and may the God of Israel grant you what you have asked of him." (Verse 17, NIV).

I know that, because of how you feel today, you may have some serious doubts that you can ever move beyond the constant state of sadness, despair and despondency that you are experiencing. I understand. I felt like that once myself too. But I'm here to confirm what God has already told you. You can and will find freedom – mental, emotional, and spiritual – from depression. You must believe that you can and you will!

God is able to do exceedingly, abundantly above all that we can ever ask or think! (*Ephesians 3:20*). In the words of Pastor John Jenkins of the First Baptist Church of Glenarden in Maryland, "God is able to take you beyond, beyond!" And while it may seem like you've been living with depression forever, you must know that God's delay doesn't mean His denial! God sees and knows all. More specifically, He knows that He can trust you with this experience. And as hard and as painful as it may be, He knows that out of your pain you can have joy! You must believe that you can and will get better.

You've got to want to live out the true purpose of your life that God has ordained for you. Within you lies a living testimony of God's undeniable power to heal and restore. Within you lies that loving mother, faithful friend, budding entrepreneur, preacher, teacher, doctor, lawyer that seemed to have disappeared into the shadows so long ago.

I Samuel 1:18 tells us that after her encounter with Eli at the temple, Hannah went her way. She left the grounds of the temple and made her way back home. Scripture also tells us that she ate – probably for the first time in weeks – and her countenance was no longer sad. We can infer that the Lord had delivered her from her depression.

Deciding that you're sick and tired of being sick and tired is a critical step to finding the freedom from depression that you need and deserve. That said, for many women overcoming depression is a process, a journey. It takes patience, determination, focus, prayer and professional help — and sometimes a long time. Give yourself permission, in advance, to have setbacks along the way. There will be days during your recovery that you won't feel like getting out of bed, eating, going to work or church, or even praying for God to help you. The key is to not stay down but to push - despite how you may feel - beyond where you are at that moment. Push past your hurt. Push past your pain. Whatever you do, keep pushing. Don't stop trying to get better. Every step forward is a step closer to your healing. You must remind yourself that depression is not your destiny.

Of course, the road to restoration is not paved with gold. There's yet another part of the healing process that we often don't talk about - the journey that you sometimes have to go through to get through and over.

I need to take you back to my cruise ship vacation for just a minute. This is such a key part of my story and my healing. After that life-changing afternoon with God, looking out at the ocean and hearing Him speak to me with that ever-clear voice, I got up from the deck of that ship with a peace in my heart that I hadn't felt in years. The Lord had taken me into

His arms, cradling me above the waves and the warmth of that salty, Caribbean sea, and promised me that I'd get me life back.

But I gotta keep this real. My life since that day on the cruise ship has not been without its share of pain and anguish. God never promised me perfection or a constant state of bliss. What He did promise me was peace and freedom from the shroud of sadness that had covered me for so many years.

I came back to my life in D.C. and to a whirlwind of change that brought both joy and sorrow. Over a five-year period, my life had become a frozen landscape with nothing moving and everything weighed down like sheets of ice. As the Lord restored my mind and then my spirit, I experienced the pain of the thaw.

Have you ever had frostbite? Or maybe just experienced the numbness that really cold weather can bring to your hands and feet? Well, if you're like me, when you get inside from being out in the cold too long and your fingers and toes begin to thaw out and warm up, there's sometimes pain. It starts out with just a slight tingle as your extremities attempt to warm themselves up again. But as the blood rushes back in and your senses re-emerge, it can be painful and overwhelming.

Unfortunately, in the years that followed my depression, I experienced the pain of separation and divorce, and the break up of my family and the home we had established. In addition,

I agonized for months over whether I should leave my cozy 9-to-5 job to pursue my consulting practice full-time, weighing the realities of exchanging a six-figure salary for the insecurity of being an entrepreneur with no guarantee for income beyond what I had managed to save. Even more difficult, I gave birth to my former husband and my third child, but this time as a single mother – not at all what I had planned. That experience alone almost sent me back into the arms of depression. Once again, I felt alone and afraid — despite having a loving circle of friends and family surrounding me. I questioned myself over and over again. I questioned my value and self-worth. My mother came to live with me to help me get back on my feet, but I felt like a child again. I had lost so much of what was important to me. My home, my marriage, the security of a high-level corporate job — and all of this in the space of two short years! I so desperately wanted to wear my strong Black woman masks again! As bad as things had been then, they seemed easier than they did at this point in my life.

Talk about the pain of the thaw! At times, it felt like searing heat and I couldn't stand the pain. I often felt like giving up! I wrestled with God over every decision – wondering if I had jumped out of the frying pan into the fire. And, despite having moved past the darkest days of my depression, I cried many days and nights. More often than I want to admit, I could feel that ugly spirit of depression lurking around, trying to find its show pain and hurt without worrying about being weak. I've learned that I must talk when I feel overwhelmed by what's going on inside of me; to do otherwise suffocates me.

I've learned to talk when I'm feeling weighed down emotionally, first to God and then to those whom I love and trust and who have my best interests at heart. I have spiritual leaders in my life whom I can trust and confide in and a very special group of close girlfriends who will listen to me without judgment. They've "talked me off the ledge" so many times. I thank God for each and every one of them!

But as painful as my depression was, it brought me a gift: It has helped me be a better person. I can now better empathize with those who are broken and in pain. I'm a better listener, friend, sister and mother for having gone through this experience. I've learned patience. I've learned what it means to have lived through the valley of the shadow of emotional and mental death. I've learned not to take life for granted. I've learned what it means to trust in God for not only my salvation but also my sanity!

I admit, in the first few years of my recovery, I struggled with where I was and where I had been. I let my voice be silenced with the weight of my growing business, personal relationships and spiritual forgetfulness. I felt guilty and ashamed for not keeping my promises to the Lord and I struggled with those feelings for a long time. Regardless of my circumstances, I know that I owe Him my life and all of the blessings He has poured into it. I owe God my eternal thanks for restoring not only my mind but also my spirit. And in the words of Co-Pastor Susie Owens of Greater Mount Calvary Holy Church in Washington, D.C., "I'm so glad I don't look like what I've been through!" I have found joy again. I have my life back!

With the help of God, I have learned that He will provide for all of my needs according to His riches in glory! I've learned to really trust and depend on Him for the success of my business. (And trust me, He has blessed me above all that I could ever ask or think!) I've learned that with His help and a determination to never go back to that depression-filled life. I *will* live and *not* die!

Now go, my sistah! Get the help that you so desperately need. Pray. Talk. Earnestly seek the Lord for deliverance from the clutches of pain and despair.

And, like Hannah, get up, go your way and eat! Sadness and depression have seen their last days in your life!

To Encourage Your *Mind*

Peace is not the absence of conflict, but the presence of God
no matter what the conflict.

~ Anonymous

There are many things that are essential to arriving at true
peace of mind, and one of the most important is faith, which
cannot be acquired without prayer.

~ John Wooden

The greater the obstacle, the more glory in overcoming it.

~ Molière

I truly believe that we can overcome any hurdle that lies
before us and create the life we want to live. I have seen it
happen time and time again.

~ Gillian Anderson

The most authentic thing about us is our capacity to create, to overcome, to endure, to transform, to love and to be greater than our suffering.

~ Ben Okri

To Encourage Your *Spirit*

Psalm 55:22

Cast thy burden upon the Lord, and he shall sustain thee: he shall never suffer the righteous to be moved.

Psalm 91:2

I will say of the Lord, He is my refuge and my fortress: my God; in him will I trust.

Isaiah 40:29

He giveth power to the faint; and to them that have no might he increaseth strength.

Isaiah 43:2

When thou passest through the waters, I will be with thee; and through the rivers, they shall not overflow thee: when though walkest through the fire, though shall not be burned; neither shall the flame kindle upon thee.

Jeremiah 29:11

For I know the thoughts that I think toward you, saith the Lord, thoughts of peace, and not of evil, to give you an expected end.

Matthew 11:28

Come unto me, all ye that labour and are heavy lade, and I will give you rest.

Luke 1:37

For with God, nothing shall be impossible.

John 14:27

Peace I leave with you, my peace I give unto you: not as the world giveth, give I unto you. Let not your heart be troubled, neither let it be afraid.

II Corinthians 3:17

Now the Lord is that Spirit: and where the Spirit of the Lord is, there is liberty.

Ephesians 3:20

Now unto him that is able to do exceeding abundantly above all that we ask or think, according to the power that worketh in us.

Philippians 4:6

Be careful for nothing: but in everything by prayer and supplication with thanksgiving let your request be known unto God. And the peace of God, which passeth all understanding, shall keep your hearts and minds through Christ Jesus.

II Timothy 1:7

For God hath not given us the spirit of fear; but of power, and of love and of a sound mind.

I Peter 5:10

But the God of all grace, who hath called us unto his eternal glory by Christ Jesus, after that ye have suffered a while, make you perfect, stablish, strengthen, settle you.

1 John 5:14-15

And this is the confidence that we have in him, that, if we ask any thing according to his will, he heareth us; And if we know that he hear us, whatsoever we ask, we know that we have the petitions that we desired of him.

Jude 1:24-25

Now unto him that his able to keep you from falling, and to present you faultless before the presence of his glory with exceeding joy, To the only wise God our Saviour, be glory and majesty, dominion and power both now and for ever.

Amen.

Appendix
Resources to Deal with Depression

National Alliance on Mental Illness   800-950-NAMI
www.nami.org

Mental Health America   800-273-TALK (8255)

National Campaign on Clinical   800-228-1114
   Depression
(a program of Delta Sigma Theta Sorority & The National Black Nurses Association)

Black Women's Health Network, www.blackwomenshealth. com

www.depressionforums.org.

Books/DVDs on Depression

Black Pain: It Just Looks Like We're Not Hurting, Terrie M. Williams, 2008

Shifting: The Double Lives of Black Women in America, Charisse Jones and Kumea Shorter-Gooden, PhD, 2003

Too Broken to Be Fixed? A Spiritual Guide to Inner Healing, Dr. Gloria Morrow, Shining Glory Publications, Inc.

Suffer in Silence No More, Dr. Gloria Morrow, DVD, http://www.gloriamorrow.com/books.html

Endnotes

[1] Fertility, Family Planning, and Reproductive Health of U.S. Women: Data From the 2002 National Survey of Family Growth

[2] National Alliance on Mental Illness, African American Women and Depression, Fact Sheet, October 2009

[3] Depression-help-resource.com

[4] National Alliance on Mental Illness, African American Women and Depression, Fact Sheet, October 2009

[5] Medicinenet.com   (http://www.medterms.com/script/main/art.asp?articlekey=9463

[6] Shifting: The Double Lives of Black Women in America, Charisse Jones and Kumea Shorter-Gooden, PhD, p. 124-126

[7] Shifting: The Double Lives of Black Women in America, Charisse Jones and Kumea Shorter-Gooden, PhD, p. 124-126

CPSIA information can be obtained
at www.ICGtesting.com
Printed in the USA
LVOW11*2313310517

536527LV00021B/759/P